FRENCH PIANO MUSIC
AN ANTHOLOGY

Edited by Isidor Philipp

Dover Publications, Inc.
New York

Published in Canada by General Publishing Company,
Ltd., 30 Lesmill Road, Don Mills, Toronto, Ontario.
Published in the United Kingdom by Constable and
Company, Ltd.

This Dover edition, first published in 1977, is a new selection
of music from the two-volume set ("Early Composers" and
"Modern Composers") originally published by the Oliver Dit-
son Company, Boston, 1906, under the title *Anthology of
French Piano Music* in the series "The Musicians Library."
The present edition is published by special arrangement with
the Theodore Presser Company, Bryn Mawr, Pennsylvania.

International Standard Book Number: 0-486-23381-2
Library of Congress Catalog Card Number: 77-75524

Manufactured in the United States of America
Dover Publications, Inc.
180 Varick Street
New York, N. Y. 10014

Contents

This 1977 edition retains the 1906 English renderings of the titles even in the few cases where they are not true translations of the French titles. The names and dates of the composers, however, now conform to the most recent biographical information, and the anthologized pieces are now arranged by the correct years of birth.

page

JACQUES CHAMPION DE CHAMBONNIÈRES (c. 1602–1672)
Canaries, in G; Gigue   1

JEAN-BAPTISTE LULLY (1632–1687; Italian, active in Paris)
Courante, in E Minor   3
Tender Melody (Air tendre)   7

ANDRÉ CAMPRA (1660–1744)
Passepied (arranged from the 1697 opera *L'Europe galante*)   9

FRANÇOIS COUPERIN (1668–1733)
Melancholy (La Lugubre); Sarabande   11
The Fickle Country-Maid (Le Bavolet flottant)   13
Butterflies (Les Papillons)   16
La Ténébreuse; Allemande   19
The Little Windmills (Les petits Moulins à vent)   21

ANDRÉ-CARDINAL DESTOUCHES (1672–1749)
Passepied in Rondeau Form (arranged from the 1697 opera *Issé*)   24
Canaries (arranged from the 1699 opera *Amadis de Grèce*)   26

JEAN-BAPTISTE LOEILLET (1680–1730; Belgian, active in London)
Sarabande, in G Minor   27
Gigue, in G Minor   28

JEAN-FRANÇOIS DANDRIEU (1682–1738)
Impatience (L'Empressée)   32

JEAN-PHILIPPE RAMEAU (1683–1764)
The Egyptian Maiden (L'Egyptienne)   34
Gavotte with Variations (Gavotte variée)   38
The Hen (La Poule)   46

FRANÇOIS DAGINCOURT (1684?–1758)
The Turtle-Doves (Les Tourterelles); Rondeau   52
The Windmill (Le Moulin à vent)   59

LOUIS-CLAUDE DAQUIN (1694–1772)
The Cuckoo (Le Coucou); Rondeau   62
Graceful Melody (La Mélodieuse); Rondeau   67

JOHANN SCHOBERT (c. 1720–1767; German, active in Paris)
Allegro Molto   71

FRANÇOIS-JOSEPH GOSSEC (1734–1829; Belgian, active in Paris)
Gavotte (arranged from the 1786 opera *Rosine*)   74

CHARLES-HENRI VALENTIN ALKAN (1813–1888)
Prelude in B Major   78
The Dying (Le Mourant) from "The Months"   80

GEORGES MATHIAS (1826–1910)
Velocity (La Vélocité)   83

CAMILLE SAINT-SAËNS (1835–1921)
Minuet (Menuet)   91
Romance [Song] Without Words (Romance sans paroles)   97

LÉO DELIBES (1836–1891)
Passepied; No. 6 from "Six Dances in the Old Style"   101

THÉODORE DUBOIS (1837–1924)
Chaconne (style panaché)   105

GEORGES BIZET (1838–1875)
The Return (Le Retour); No. 6 from "Songs of the Rhine"   110

EMMANUEL CHABRIER (1841–1894)
Scherzo-Valse; No. 10 from "Picturesque Pieces"   117

JULES MASSENET (1842–1912)
Toccata   126

CHARLES-MARIE WIDOR (1844–1937)
Valse-Impromptu   132
At Evening (Au Soir)   137

GABRIEL FAURÉ (1845–1924)
Romance [Song] Without Words (Romance sans paroles)   140
Fourth Barcarolle (Quatrième Barcarolle)   143

BENJAMIN GODARD (1849–1895)
Pan; No. 2 from "The Magic Lantern," Part I   149
Running (En courant); No. 1 from "On the Road"   154

VINCENT D'INDY (1851–1931)
Scherzo from the Sonata in C   164

CÉCILE CHAMINADE (1857–1944)
Sea Piece (Marine)   171

CAMILLE ERLANGER (1863–1919)
Album Leaf (Feuillet d'album)   177

GABRIEL PIERNÉ (1863–1937)
In the Church (A l'Eglise); Choral   180

ISIDOR PHILIPP (1863–1958)
Caprice   183

CANARIES, in G

GIGUE

Edited by *Isidor Philipp*

JACQUES CHAMPION de CHAMBONNIÈRES

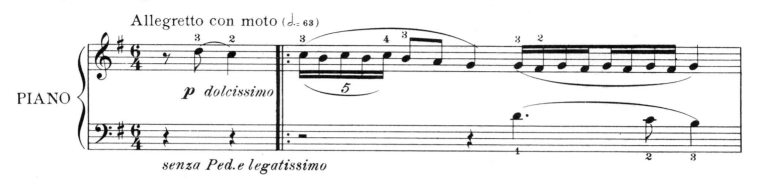

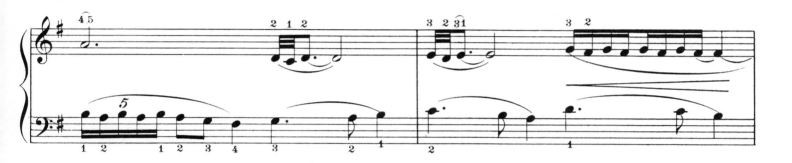

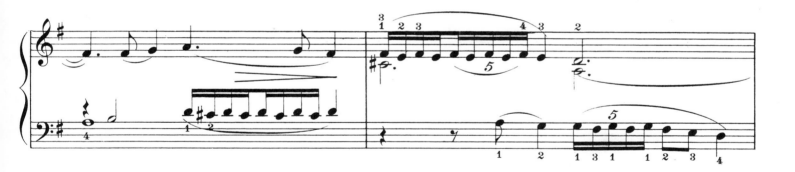

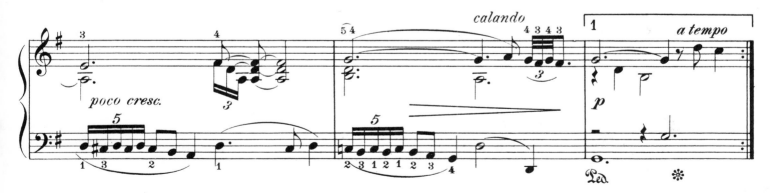

Grace and naïveté are the leading characteristics of this little piece. It should be played softly and delicately throughout. The pedal may be employed *una corda*.

Le caractère prédominant de cette petite pièce est la grace et la naïveté. Elle doit être jouée d'un bout à l'autre avec la plus grande douceur. On peut employer la pédale una corda.

COURANTE, in E Minor

Edited by *Isidor Philipp*

JEAN-BAPTISTE LULLY

TENDER MELODY
(AIR TENDRE)

Edited by Isidor Philipp

JEAN-BAPTISTE LULLY

The **rendering** of this little piece demands a touch of the utmost delicacy.

L'exécution de cette pièce exige un toucher d'une extrème délicatesse.

GENTLE EUROPA
(L' EUROPE GALANTE)

PASSEPIED

Edited by Isidor Philipp

ANDRÉ CAMPRA

MELANCHOLY
(LA LUGUBRE)
SARABANDE

Edited by Isidor Philipp

FRANÇOIS COUPERIN

To realize the tragic nature of this composition demands an interpretation both simple and broad – almost in the style of lyric declamation.

Pour rendre le caractère tragique de cette admirable pièce, il faut une interprétation simple et large – presque de la déclamation lyrique.

THE FICKLE COUNTRY-MAID
(LE BAVOLET FLOTTANT)

Edited by Isidor Philipp

FRANÇOIS COUPERIN

Allegro teneramente, leggiero e legato (♩.=63-66)

BUTTERFLIES
(LES PAPILLONS)

Edited by Isidor Philipp

FRANÇOIS COUPERIN

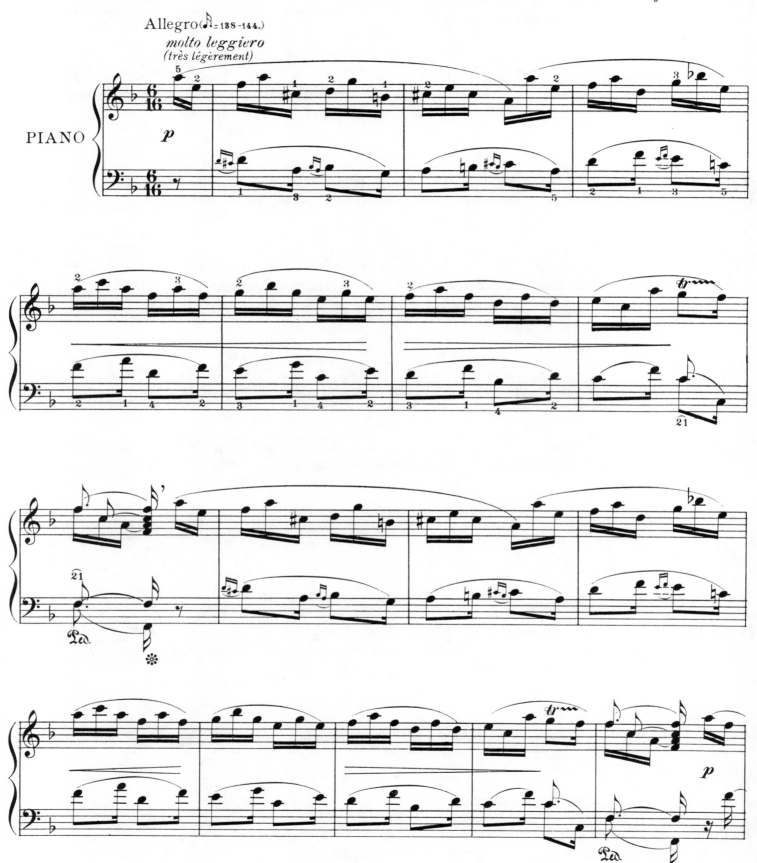

LA TÉNÉBREUSE
ALLEMANDE

Edited by Isidor Philipp

FRANÇOIS COUPERIN

THE LITTLE WINDMILLS
(LES PETITS MOULINS À VENT)

Edited by Isidor Philipp

FRANÇOIS COUPERIN

ISSÉ

PASSEPIED IN RONDEAU FORM

Edited by Isidor Philipp

ANDRÉ DESTOUCHES

The Passepied is a sort of minuet in rapid movement, and bearing a resemblance to the Courante.

Le passepieds est une espèce de menuet très-vif ayant de l'analogie avec la courante.

AMADIS OF GREECE
(AMADIS DE GRÈCE)
CANARIES

Edited by Isidor Philipp

ANDRÉ DESTOUCHES

The Canarie was a species of the old gigue, but slower.

Les Canaries sont une espèce de gigue ancienne lente.

SARABANDE, in G Minor

Edited by Isidor Philipp

JEAN-BAPTISTE LOEILLET

GIGUE, in G Minor

Edited by Isidor Philipp

JEAN-BAPTISTE LOEILLET

Molto vivace (♩.=138)
(non legato)

PIANO

IMPATIENCE
(L' EMPRESSÉE)

Edited by Isidor Philipp

JEAN-FRANÇOIS DANDRIEU

THE EGYPTIAN MAIDEN
(L' ÉGYPTIENNE)

Edited by *Isidor Philipp*

JEAN-PHILIPPE RAMEAU

GAVOTTE WITH VARIATIONS
(GAVOTTE VARIÉE)

Edited by Isidor Philipp

JEAN-PHILIPPE RAMEAU

40

DOUBLE IV (♩=144)

brillante con bravura

DOUBLE VI

Sostenuto (♩=108)

la seconda volta **pp** *(una corda)*

THE HEN
(LA POULE)

Edited by Isidor Philipp

JEAN-PHILIPPE RAMEAU

THE TURTLE-DOVES
(LES TOURTERELLES)
RONDEAU

Edited by Isidor Philipp

FRANÇOIS DAGINCOURT

Maggiore

cresc.

dim.

pp espressivo

una corda sin'al Fine

tr

THE WINDMILL
(LE MOULIN À VENT)

Edited by Isidor Philipp

FRANÇOIS DAGINCOURT

PIANO

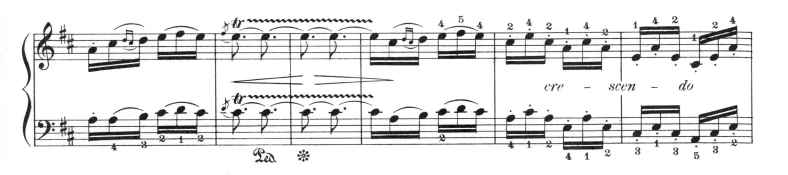

THE CUCKOO
(LE COUCOU)

RONDEAU

Edited by Isidor Philipp

LOUIS-CLAUDE DAQUIN

Brisk and sprightly tempo, clean attack, careful observation of nuances—these are the requisite qualities for an adequate interpretation of this delicate fancy of Daquin.

Allure vive et enjouée, attaque légère, nuances finement ménagées, voilà ce qu'il faut à l'interprétation de cette spirituelle page de Daquin.

GRACEFUL MELODY
(LA MÉLODIEUSE)

RONDEAU

Edited by Isidor Philipp

LOUIS-CLAUDE DAQUIN

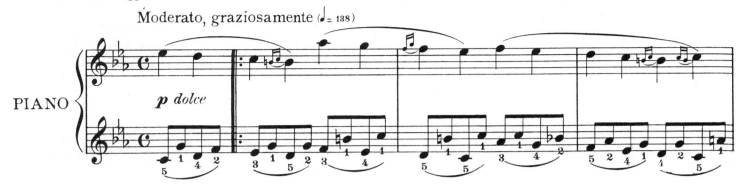

COUPLET I

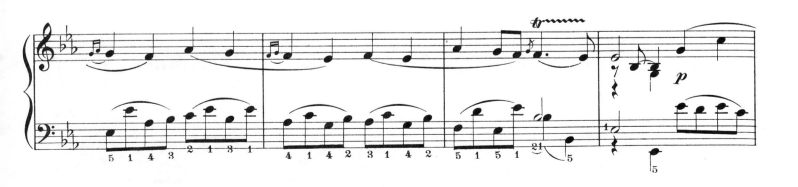

COUPLET II

ALLEGRO MOLTO

Edited by *Isidor Philipp*

JOHANN SCHOBERT

una corda

tre corde

ROSINE

GAVOTTE

Edited by *Isidor Philipp*

FRANÇOIS GOSSEC

PRELUDE in B Major

Edited by Isidor Philipp

CHARLES VALENTIN ALKAN, Op. 31, №23

THE DYING
(LE MOURANT)
From "THE MONTHS"

Edited by Isidor Philipp

CHARLES VALENTIN ALKAN

VELOCITY
(LA VÉLOCITÉ)

Edited by Isidor Philipp

GEORGES MATHIAS

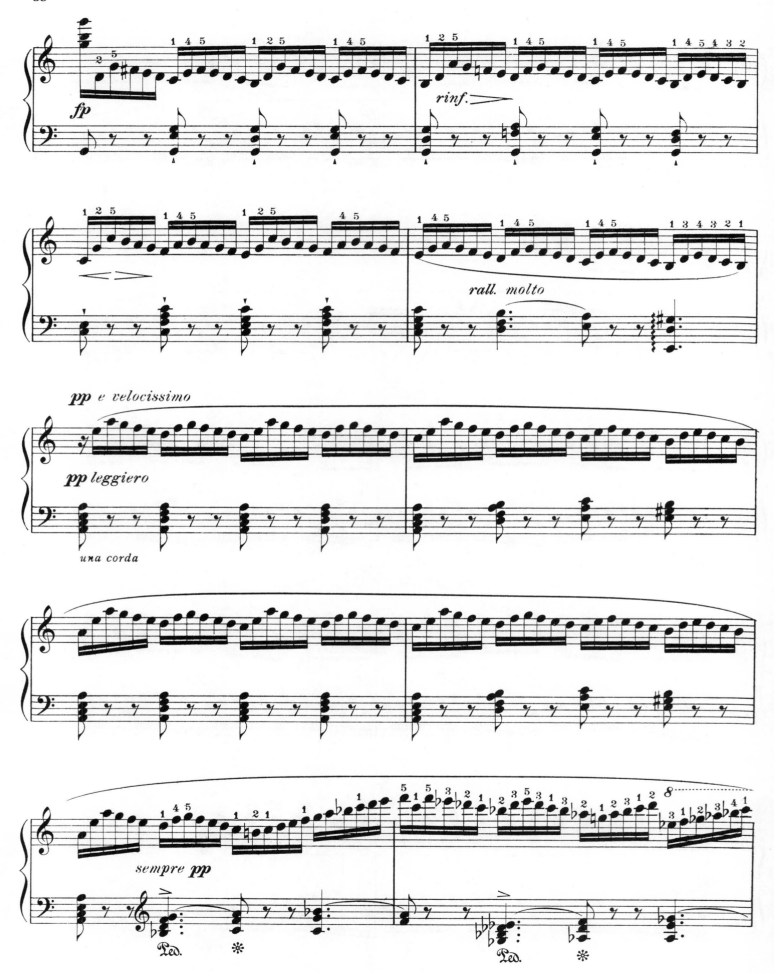

To Madame Félix Lévy

MINUET
(MENUET)

Edited by Isidor Philipp

CAMILLE SAINT-SAËNS, Op.56

Tempo di Minuetto moderato (♩= 104)

PIANO

ROMANCE WITHOUT WORDS
(ROMANCE SANS PAROLES)

Edited by Isidor Philipp

CAMILLE SAINT-SAËNS

PASSEPIED

Nº 6 from "SIX DANCES IN THE OLD STYLE"

Edited by Isidor Philipp

LÉO DELIBES

CHACONNE
(STYLE PANACHÉ)

Edited by Isidor Philipp

THÉODORE DUBOIS

To Camille Saint-Saëns

THE RETURN
(LE RETOUR)

Nº 6 from "SONGS OF THE RHINE"

Edited by Isidor Philipp

GEORGES BIZET

Le jour fuit; sur le Rhin la nuit étend ses voiles;
Il est doux de chanter et de vivre aux étoiles;
Les nuits sont, en été, plus belles que les jours—
Demain, ô jeunes gens, vous redirez encore
Votre salut au fleuve, et votre hymne à l'aurore;
Imitez votre Rhin, le Rhin chante toujours.

Joseph Méry (1798-1866).

Day dies; and o'er the Rhine night spreads her sable wing:
'Tis sweet to live and love, and 'neath the stars to sing.
The summer night is wondrous, more beautiful than day—
Yet when night wanes, O youths, you shall repeat at morn
Your greetings to the river, your homage to the dawn;
Be guided by the Rhine, which chants its song alway.

Translated by C. F. M.

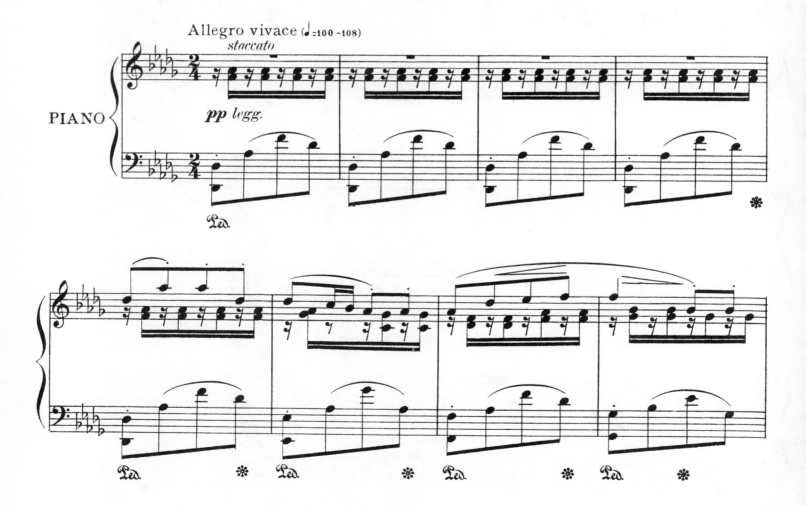

To Mlle Mina de Gabriac

SCHERZO-VALSE

Nº 10 from "PICTURESQUE PIECES"

Edited by Isidor Philipp

EMMANUEL CHABRIER

TOCCATA

Philipp

JULES MASSENET

VALSE - IMPROMPTU

Isidor Philipp

CHARLES M. WIDOR, Op.15, No 6

PIANO

AT EVENING
(AU SOIR)

Edited by Isidor Philipp

CHARLES M. WIDOR, Op.44, № 5

Andante cantabile, quasi Adagio ($\quarternote$ = 72)

Tempo I

To Madame Florent Saglio

ROMANCE WITHOUT WORDS
(ROMANCE SANS PAROLES)

Edited by Isidor Philipp

GABRIEL FAURÉ, Op. 17, № 3

To Madame Ernest Chausson

FOURTH BARCAROLLE
(QUATRIÈME BARCAROLLE)

Edited by Isidor Philipp

GABRIEL FAURÉ, Op. 44

To Madame Laure Jacquard

PAN

№ 2 from "THE MAGIC LANTERN," Part I

Edited by Isidor Philipp

BENJAMIN GODARD, Op. 50, № 2

To Mlle Suzanne Robin

RUNNING
(EN COURANT)

№ 1 from "ON THE ROAD"

Edited by Isidor Philipp

BENJAMIN GODARD, Op. 53, № 1

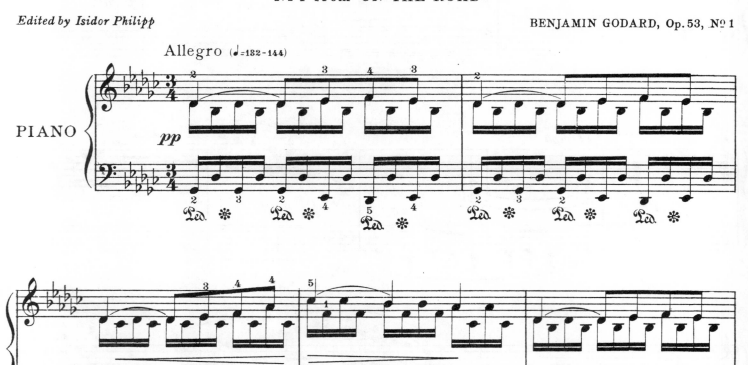

To Isidor Philipp

SCHERZO

from the **SONATA** in C.

Edited by Isidor Philipp

VINCENT D'INDY, Op. 9, № 3

Allegro non troppo (♩.= 69)

PIANO

poco *cresc.*

poco più ***f***

poco riten. *a tempo*

dim.

To Madame Jean Richepin

SEA PIECE
(MARINE)

Le temps que j'ai passé sur tes flots, mer jolie,
  Reste cher à mon cœur comme son meilleur temps,
Je ne l'oublierai pas, quand je vivrais cent ans,
  Et la douceur en moi n'en peut être abolie.

Jean Richepin

The hours I have spent on thy bosom, O sea,
  By memories fond are endeared to my heart;
Their life-giving sweetness will never depart,
  Though years a full hundred shall pass over me.

Translated by C. F. M.

Edited by Isidor Philipp

CÉCILE CHAMINADE, Op. 38

To my friend Isidor Philipp

ALBUM LEAF
(FEUILLET D'ALBUM)

Edited by Isidor Philipp

CAMILLE ERLANGER

To Madame Montigny-Rémaury

IN THE CHURCH
(À L' ÉGLISE)
CHORAL

Edited by Isidor Philipp

GABRIEL PIERNÉ, Op. 3, № 8

To E. M. Delaborde

CAPRICE

Edited by Isidor Philipp

ISIDOR PHILIPP, Op. 21